CHURCH UNITY
SERIES

REPAIRERS

OF THE

BREACH

*Truths compiled
from the writings of*

FRANCIS
FRANGIPANE

*A HOUSE
DIVIDED
CANNOT STAND*

ISBN #1-886296-05-7

CONTENTS

1.

THE SON'S ANSWERED PRAYER

*If you believe in Christ, and believe He is the only begotten of the Father, then be assured, Jesus will have all His prayers answered. A time is coming, and now is, when both heaven and earth shall respond to Jesus' prayer, **"that they may all be one"** (John 17:21).*

Jesus: the Same Forever

On the night before He died, the most somber night in Jesus' life, the Lord brought His most lofty request to God. He prayed for oneness in His church. Christ's prayer is both visionary and practical considering that, this same evening, an argument arose among His disciples as to which of them was the greatest (see Luke 22:24). In spite of their immaturity, selfish ambitions, and envy, Jesus harbored no second thoughts or unbelief when He prayed that they may all be one.

Even as the Son of God appealed for them, be assured He is praying for us now. Jesus is the same **"yesterday and today, yes and forever"** (Heb 13:8). He will never lower His standards (see John 12:48), He will not modify His promises (see Matthew 24:35), and His intercession will remain unfailing until we attain His goal for us in God (see Romans 8:34).

To know Christ is to know His heart toward His church. Look again at His relationship with His disciples that Passover night. If an observer compared the instructions of Christ with the responses of His disciples, he would have concluded that there was little communication between them. Jesus presented His vision of a church motivated by His love and humility. In contrast, His disciples dwelt in carnal desires and weaknesses.

Consider: While Jesus prayed they would be **"perfected in unity"** (John 17:23), the only unity the disciples knew that night was a common fear and a collective abandonment of Christ. Consider: Jesus told these soon-to-be leaders of the Jerusalem church that they would be known for their untiring agape love. But that night Christ's three closest friends could not remain awake with him even one hour while He agonized alone in prayer.

His disciples were deaf to His promises, blind to His sacrifice, and ignorant of His vision; they were without revelation, obedience, or courage. Yet, in spite of themselves, Jesus told these very men, **"He who believes in Me, the works that I do shall he do also; and greater works than these shall he do"** (John 14:12).

How could they ever attain His works? Oh, the grace and love of Jesus! They would do His works because He was about to **"go to the Father"** (v 12), where He would ever live to make intercession for them!

There have always existed two realms in the definition of the church: one, the place of beginnings, the disciple's world, cluttered with human fears and worldly ambitions. The second reality is the place of destination, the eternal, glorious realm which Jesus died to give us. The living span bridging both is Christ's cross and intercession. *Any time the church awakens to the promises of God, the way to holiness and power is already there. Christians must only agree with the Father's plan.*

The shallow, immature level of the church has never stopped Christ from praying for its perfection. He could no sooner stop praying than cease being the Son of God. Jesus is the Redeemer of mankind. Even in wrath, His motive is redemption!

Christ's Commitment to His Church

Jesus has always known the frailty of His church. He knows that when we commit our lives to Him, it is not a commitment that says, *"I will never sin again, I will always be good."* Try as we may, if we could keep such a resolution, we would not have needed Christ to save us!

Our salvation is not built upon what we do, but upon who Jesus becomes to us. Our commitment to Him is an acknowledgment that we have come to the end of ourselves: We *need* a savior. Having thus discovered no righteousness within us, we have entrusted both our condition and our future to Him. We commit ourselves to obeying Him, but we frequently fail. We are required to know His Word, but we barely understand it. We pledge ourselves to follow, but how often we find ourselves lost!

Our salvation is an abandonment to *His ability* to keep that which we have committed unto Him (see Philippians 1:6). He who thinks otherwise has never come face to face with his need for God. As the Lord's church, we must each discover the sustaining and renewing power of Christ's prayer. Without such knowledge, we will be overwhelmed by the many times we fail.

Peter discovered Christ's unchanging commitment that last night. Though others failed, Peter boasted of his commitment; he would not fail. However,

Jesus told His upstart disciple how, that very night, he would deny His Lord three times. Not only did Peter fail, but all Christ's disciples deserted Him that night. What was the Lord's reaction? Did He chasten Peter? Express His personal offense, or shame him? No. Although there *are* times when Christ must rebuke us, Jesus prayed that, though Peter would fail, his faith would continue, and he would be a strength to his brothers (see Luke 22:32).

Immediately after warning Peter of his impending denial (see John 13:38), Jesus further comforted His disciples. He encouraged them, **"Let not your heart be troubled; believe in God, believe also in Me"** (John 14:1). While this verse is suitable for calming any troubled heart, Jesus was speaking uniquely and compassionately to His disciples. Incredibly, it was Jesus, about to go to the cross, who comforted the very disciples who were about to deny Him!

We do not truly know Christ until we have failed and find Him still our friend, drawn ever closer to us by our repentance and our need. What is true concerning His devotion to us as individuals is true concerning His commitment to a repentant citywide church as well. Our failings have not disqualified us from God's purposes. If we turn and trust Him again, we will find that the same Lord who requires we obey Him remains our Redeemer and Intercessor when we fail Him.

Notes

The Father's Unchanging Purpose

There are two things greater, more enduring, than the failings of the church. According to Scripture, these two things are **"the unchangeableness of** [God's] **purpose"** and Christ's **"permanent"** priestly intercession (see Hebrews 6:17; 7:24).

Jesus, intimately familiar with the holy intentions of the Father, knows that it is *not* God's will for the church to be fearful, ambitious, or jealous. Christ can pray with confidence for divine love, unity, and glory to adorn His church, for these *are* God's will.

Jesus' prayers are always answered because He only prays for what is already in the Father's heart. The confidence of Christ's prayer is based upon His own personal virtue, not that of the church. Through His sacrifice, He is able **"to save forever** (lit: *"to the uttermost"*) **those who draw near to God through Him"** (Heb 7:25). Thus, the price has been paid, not only to bring us to heaven when we die, but to bring the life of heaven here where we live.

It seems that the Lord's disciples frequently carried the burden of wrong attitudes and aberrant concepts. Yet, in spite of their immaturity, Jesus unhesitantly prayed for the most holy of possibilities: that they would become the human abode for the Trinity of God—a promise which was almost blasphemous to an Old Testament mind! (John 14:16-17, 23)

When we unite with Christ in His purpose and His prayer, eternal life is released for our needs on earth. His prayer is the water that flows from the throne of God; He is the river of life which sustains and directs every move of God. No soul is saved that He has not first died for; no relationship is healed but what comes forth originally from His intervention.

What happens when we agree with Christ in prayer? As we persevere, a circuit of life is completed between heaven and earth. Christ's prayer carries us into the provision of God; our prayer, *united with His,* brings God's provision back to the need. The revivals and harvests we see emerging around the world, the collapse of communism, and the exodus of Jews back to Israel were all birthed as individuals agreed with the intercession of Christ and the plan of God.

Do we truly believe what God has provided for us in holiness, power, and glory? If so, let us persevere with Christ in confidence, knowing that all the Father has given shall be brought to earth through prayer.

2.

Repairers of the Breach

The Gathering Together of the Saints

> "And those from among you will rebuild the ancient ruins; You will raise up the age-old foundations; and you will be called the repairer of the breach, the restorer of the streets in which to dwell" (Isa 58:12).

Most of true Christianity shares a doctrine commonly called the "rapture" of the church (see 1 Thessalonians 4:16). While study and debate surround the timing of this event, Scripture assures us it will occur before Jesus Himself returns.

However, before the rapture occurs, there will be a time of unusual grace in which the living church of Jesus Christ, like a bride, makes **"herself ready"** (see Revelation 19:7). In this unparalleled season of preparation, those who are alive in Christ shall realize a level of holiness and blamelessness of the quality in which Jesus Himself walked (see 1 Thessalonians 3:11-13; Ephesians 5:26-27; Philippians 1:9-10).

The result of this new level of holiness will be a new level of unity. Fault-finding and gossip will disappear. In their place will be intercession and love. Wholeness will return to the church. This also means that the ambition and division we see today between congregations will be identified as sin, which will be repented of before Jesus returns.

The truth of this message must be made clear, for most Christians consider oneness within the body inconceivable before Jesus returns. They have not discerned nor warred against the spirit of antichrist, which conditions believers to accept strife and sectarianism in the church. *The church which will ultimately be raptured will be a church free of strife and carnal divisions.*

During the rapture, our bodies will be changed. But our *character,* that is, the essence of who we have become, will remain intact. There will be no regrets or wondering how "those from that church" made it, for the living bride will have become a church built together in love, meeting in separate buildings but serving the single Lord. The true disciples of the Lord Jesus will be known for their intense and holy love for one another—not merely in their individual local assemblies, but within the context of a citywide church.

It is highly significant that the scriptural term for the rapture is called **"the gathering together"** (2 Thess 2:1; see also Matthew 24:31). What ultimately will be consummated in our gathering together *physically* to the Lord will be precipitated by a *spiritual* gathering together of His body on earth. Concerning the "end of the age," Jesus taught that the **"good fish"** shall be **"gathered . . . into containers"** (Matt 13:48). And in the context of spiritual warfare, Jesus warned, **"he who does not gather with Me scatters"** (Matt 12:30).

This scattering, dividing process among the Lord's sheep has gone on long enough. Jesus has set His heart to bring healing and unity to His body. In this regard, through the prophet Jeremiah, the Lord spoke a somber warning. He said, **"Woe to the shepherds who are destroying and scattering the sheep of My pasture!"** (Jer 23:1) Jesus is not pleased with the carnal divisions in His body! Indeed, there will be a time of punishment, and that soon coming, in which the Lord will chasten those pastors who continue to build their kingdoms without laboring together to build His. To them He says, **"I am about to attend to you for the evil of your deeds"** (v 2).

In the tenth chapter of John, the Lord makes His goal clear: there shall be **"one flock with one shepherd"** (v 16). He reveals that it is the wolf nature which **"snatches** [the sheep], **and scatters them"** (v 12), and it is the hireling nature which allows the scattering to occur. But His promise to His sheep says this:

> **"Then I Myself shall gather the remnant of My flock . . . and they will be fruitful and multiply. I shall also raise up shepherds over them and they will tend them; and they will not be afraid any longer . . . nor will any be missing"** (Jer 23:3-4).

The pastors of the last Christian church will be undershepherds to the Lord Jesus; they will be anointed to gather together His remnant and under that anointing shall be **"fruitful and multiply."**

Indeed, right now, in the context of humbling ourselves and submitting our hearts to His will, we are participating in being "gathered together." And that process will progressively increase until the barriers between brethren are melted by the overcoming nature of Christ's love. Before Jesus returns, we will truly be **"one flock with one shepherd."** We will be a holy and blameless sheepfold, meeting in different buildings but baptized into one body.

Do not Criticize the Breach; Repair it!

> **Thus says the Lord God, "Woe to the foolish prophets who are following their own spirit and have seen nothing. O Israel, your prophets have been like foxes among ruins. You have not gone up into the breaches, nor did you build the wall around the house of Israel to stand in the battle on the day of the Lord"** (Ezek 13:3-5).

God needs people who, when they see a gap in the citywide church wall, will go up into the breaches and rebuild the wall, so that the church will stand in the day of battle. In every city, town, and village, you need the other churches if you are going to stand in the day of battle.

You may be thinking, "You don't understand, I have revelation of the end-time move of God. These churches barely believe in Jesus." The Word tells us that, **"without any dispute the lesser is blessed by the greater"** (Heb 7:7). If you are truly **"greater"** you will seek ways to be a blessing to other churches. Your Christlike love will cast out fears. You will truly have a burden to see the entire body of Christ brought forth, not just your local assembly. In truth, Jesus said that the greatest among us would become the

"servant of *all*" (Mark 9:35; see also Matthew 23:11).

If a church in your city holds to and confesses Jesus, you need each other, and you must serve each other to complete God's work there. As you join one another for daily or weekly prayer, you will be surprised by God's preparation of His people. Do not come with an attitude to teach or lead, but to love and serve. In this, God is not looking for leaders, but *followers* of the Lord Jesus Christ.

If we do not adjust to His will, we will be unable to stand against the enemy. Indeed, the day in which we live is not a day of peace, it is a time of war. God is gathering us together not only to Him and to each other, but also against the spiritual forces of wickedness in every region. Therefore, the breaches between us must be filled, the walls built, and we must learn to stand together in the day of the Lord.

You Be the People

You do not have to go to college to find fault with the church. In fact, if you remember, you could find fault with the church even before you were a Christian. You do not need skill to find fault. But if you want to be like Christ, you have to die for people's sins. You have to be an intercessor who "stands in the gap." *The "gap" is the distance between the way things are and the way things should be.* You stand in that space, cast down the

Notes

accuser of the brethren, and intercede! Have you seen something that is wrong? it is only because Jesus wants you to stand in the gap and see it changed. That is the only reason.

Some of us have cried for years, "Where are the men to lead us into Christ's fullness?" We have assumed that God had others in mind for His purposes. What the Lord is saying, however, is, *"You be the men and women that others are looking for."* You be the peacemakers, the sons of God, that bring healing and order to His church.

The responsibility is upon each of us. There is a tremendous job ahead, but the Lord Himself has promised,

> **those from among you will rebuild the ancient ruins; you will raise up the age-old foundations; and you will be called the repairer of the breach, the restorer of the paths in which to dwell** (Isa 58:12).

Let us lay our lives down in committed faith that, in our lifetimes, on this earth, and in our communities, the corporate church of Jesus Christ will be restored, united, and holy!

3.

WHEN THE LORD BUILDS HIS HOUSE

It is possible for Christ's church to be so properly aligned with heaven that the Holy Spirit actually displaces the powers of darkness over our cities. To the degree that the church is so joined to God, the Lord's presence guards the city: crime and immorality proportionally decline; revival breaks out. But be forewarned: Only if the Lord builds His house will He then guard our cities (see Psalm 127:1).

The Corporate, Citywide Church

And the house, while it was being built, was built of stone prepared at the

quarry" (1 Kings 6:7). During these past years God has had His church **"at the quarry"** shaping the leaders, preparing their hearts to become part of the house of the Lord. Under the hammer of the Word, many pastors and lay people have had their rock-hard religious and doctrinal opinions shattered. God has been reducing their definition of Christianity to the biblical proportions of **"simplicity and purity of devotion to Christ"** (2 Cor 11:3). At the same time the Lord has also laid His axe to the root system of **"jealousy and selfish ambition"** (James 3:16).

All across the world men and women of God are being fitted together into a living temple for the Lord. Burning in their hearts is a new vision for a united church. Together with their congregations, these servants of God are building their churches, not upon the typical American base of self-promotion and human enterprise, but upon a substructure of corporate, citywide prayer and Christian love. With great passion and deep humility, their singular goal is to see Christ Himself formed in the church (see Galatians 4:19). In so doing, they are laying the foundation for the house of the Lord.

It is a testimony to Christ's wisdom and power how graciously these "living stones" accept one another and fit together. These men and women, often of very different church backgrounds, are finding themselves kneeling in one another's buildings and praying at each other's side. Their common prayer is that the Almighty might unite them in Christ and finish the house of the Lord—that Christ Himself might heal their cities.

God will answer their prayers. The house of the Lord is beginning to emerge upon the building site of the praying, citywide church. The time of devastation and shaping, of being hammered and cut to size, is nearly over. The day of power is at hand.

The Obedience of Christ

This is not a work born out of compromise. It would be an error to assume the goal of this move of God is unity. No, our objective is obedience. Out of obedience to God in prayer and true desire to be Christlike, a new meaning to unity has come.

Our focus is upon Christ. Paul instructed the church to take **"every thought captive to the obedience of Christ"** (2 Cor 10:5). The areas of our thought life which are not captive to Christ are the areas where we are losing our battle against hell. But when our vision is focused upon the Lord and becoming like Him in obedience, the conclusion of what Paul wrote will be fulfilled: **"And we are ready to punish all disobedience, whenever your obedience is complete"** (2 Cor 10:6).

It would be presumption to speculate on all this verse means. We know that Paul was not referring to flesh and blood; he was not warring according to the flesh (see Eph 6:12). The implication here is that when the obedience of the church is made complete, there will be an unleashing of the mightiest display of spiritual power the world has ever seen.

This revelation of power was *not* attained in Paul's day. The provision was there in that the prince of this world was "judged," "rendered powerless," and "disarmed" at the cross, but obviously "all disobedience" was not punished in the first century.

Let us ask the Lord Himself: Is there something yet to come through the obedient church that will bring judgment upon spiritual wickedness and disobedience and also deliver many cities?

When the Lord Guards the City

"Unless the Lord builds the house, they labor in vain who build it; unless the Lord guards the city, the watchman keeps awake in vain" (Ps 127:1). Before we discuss this verse it is important to explain a characteristic often found in the Hebrew Scriptures. Often the Old Testament writers communicated truth by repeating two views of the same thought. We see this especially in Psalms and Proverbs. An example would be: **"With the fruit of a man's mouth his stomach**

will be satisfied; he will be satisfied with the product of his lips" (Prov 18:20). The same concept is presented twice in two ways. Another example is: **"I will open my mouth in a parable; I will utter dark sayings of old"** (Ps 78:2). Truth is conveyed using a poetic rhythm that is both beautiful and functional—a way of compressing two corresponding thoughts into one idiom.

In this regard, when the psalmist admonishes, **"Unless the Lord builds the house, they labor in vain who build it; unless the Lord guards the city, the watchman keeps awake in vain"** (Ps 127:1), he is saying the same truth in two ways. The work of the Lord is a bridge connecting these two thoughts: the house He builds will stand; the city He guards will be protected.

How can the Lord guard the city? The house of the Lord is a house of prayer; intercession brings the presence of God into the city. Let me say this another way: *When* the Lord builds the house, *then* the Lord will guard the city. The specifications of His building plans require His people to be praying, loving and investing themselves into their cities, and empowered by His anointing. The house of the Lord will change our communities!

Jesus confirms this in His promise that **"I will build My church; and the gates of hell shall not prevail against it"** (Matt 16:18 KJV). He is stating that when His house is built in obedience to His

Word, the strongholds of evil over individuals and cities will be broken.

When there is revival in a city, what happens to the powers of darkness in the heavenly places? Where do they go? They are displaced by the fullness of God's Spirit in the regional church. Paul tells us that it is **"through the church"** that the manifold wisdom of God is revealed **"to the rulers and the authorities in the heavenly places"** (Eph 3:10). And what is happening in the spirit realm? The church is blessed with **"every spiritual blessing in the heavenly places in Christ"** (Eph 1:3). The prevailing influence upon society in this case comes from heaven; the Lord guards the city!

When the church is not built according to Christ's directives but remains selfish and divided, the principalities and powers have access in a greater degree to the souls of men. In such cities, spiritual wickedness guards the city.

One does not have to be very discerning to see this is true. On your next drive from the country into a city, you may notice a distinguishable cloud of oppression as you enter the city. That invisible barrier marks the influence of the ruling spirits of the community. The demonic power of that area is the **"strong man, fully armed,"** who **"guards his own homestead,"** whose **"possessions are undisturbed"** (Luke 11:21).

But when the church is obedient to Christ, it will be united with other believers and unstoppable by the powers of hell. Through the church and its prayer, love, and action, the Lord will guard the city.

Whatever You Bind Will Be Bound

Let me explain the interaction between the spirit world and the thoughts and actions of men. As I see it, the spirit realm can be accessed and occupied by either angels or demons, depending upon the attitude of man. Although the earth is the Lord's, He put all things under man's feet—that is, under man's responsibility.

When Satan told Jesus that all the world and its glory have **"been handed over to me"** (Luke 4:6), he was speaking a half-truth. The world has indeed been given to the devil, not by God, but by man!

We have wrongly assumed that the devil has divine approval to attack our neighborhoods and cities. Satan has access to the domain of darkness, but he can only occupy those areas where mankind, through sin, has allowed him to occupy.

Thus, Jesus tells the church, **"whatever you shall bind on earth shall be bound in heaven, and whatever you shall loose on earth shall be loosed in heaven"** (Matt 16:19; see also 18:18). Notice that Jesus gave the same instruction for two seemingly different situations. The context of Matthew 16:18-19 deals with the devil, while the focus of Matthew 18:15-18 is sin. These realms are interconnected. The sinfulness of mankind—his evil thoughts, words, and actions—is the very shelter of the devil over our cities! Since this is true, then righteousness in the church proportionally displaces the devil in the spirit realm, offering Satan no hiding place. He may tempt, but he cannot abide. Indeed, when the church truly draws near to God, the devil flees.

A New Vision

If we work together to build the house of the Lord, our strengths will be amplified rather than diminished. One of the pastors in my city has been used by God to picket abortion clinics and stores which sell pornography. Before the churches began to pray together, the most he ever mustered for a protest were 120 people. However, because a larger number of churches are united with him now in prayer, over four thousand people came recently to stand against abortion! Since then the local television stations and newspapers have been far more sympathetic to the cause of the unborn.

Where the churches are united, the benefit upon teens will be wonderful. Imagine how it would be if there were a citywide youth group where large numbers of Christian teens could meet and unite. Older teens could develop leadership skills and pastoral care over younger teenagers.

Without limiting their overseas missions, pastors are realizing that the first mission field they need to support is the local one. Ministers in churches are beginning to build together, training individuals from their congregations to go to other churches in the city, where together the entire local Christian community is being built up.

Ultimately, how will the house of the Lord differ from current Christianity? Although the Lord has visited the church with revival in the past, He will dwell in power in His house. Healing and deliverance will be commonplace; holiness and grace will fill the atmosphere. Where the house of the Lord is built, the protection of the Lord will be felt.

A Living Testimony

Our ministry is located in Cedar Rapids, Iowa. When we first started praying together with other pastors and intercessors in the city, the state of Iowa was experiencing an 11 percent increase in violent crime. During this same time, however, in Cedar Rapids violent crime *decreased* 17 percent. FBI files confirm that Cedar Rapids became the safest city of over 100,000 people in the United States in 1988. In spite of the enemy's counterattack, Cedar Rapids remains one of the safest cities in the nation. We

Notes

continue to experience many wonderful and significant breakthroughs in our city.

To the degree that the Lord's house is established in our cities, lawlessness will proportionally decrease. The time is soon upon us when, unless we are building the Lord's house, our labors may actually be in vain. But the Holy Spirit's encouragement to us is unwavering: When the Lord builds the house, then the Lord will guard the city.

Lord, thank You for Your dealings in my life. Thank You for shaping my heart to fit in with other believers in my city. O God, increase Your work in this region until Your entire church is one body, one force, one weapon in Your hand against evil! Build and then enter Your house, Lord Jesus. Open the door of Your house, and step onto our streets. Guard our cities with power. In Jesus' name. Amen.